DATE			

WHY DO WE HAVE HALLOWEEN?

BY

LINDELL HAGAN EDWARDS

A Bookland Juvenile

Carlton Press Corp.   New York, N.Y.

ACKNOWLEDGMENT

I wish to acknowledge my parents, Lindel Hagan and Colene Willett Hagan, for their support and encouragement in all my writing endeavors.

ACKNOWLEDGMENT

I wish to acknowledge my parents, Lindell Hagan and Colette (Wright) Hagan for their support and encouragement in all my own endeavors.

*This book is dedicated
to my wonderful husband, Jerry,
who has been most supportive of my writing endeavors.*

*To all of my Irish Ancestors,
from whom I received the Irish Tales.*

*To all of my former students,
who inspired me to write the book,
by asking the question,
"Why do we have Halloween?"*

*To my granddaughter, Jessica,
who read the book through a child's eyes
and said, "Gee, Mom, that's a good book!
I didn't know just a normal person like you could write a book!"*

WHY DO WE HAVE

HALLOWEEN?

Halloween is always on October thirty-first.

OCTOBER

Sun	Mon	Tue	Wed	Thu	Fri	Sat
1	2	3	4	5	6	7
8	9	10	11	12	13	14
15	16	17	18	19	20	21
22	23	24	25	26	27	28
29	30	31				

SEPTEMBER						
S	M	T	W	T	F	S
					1	2
3	4	5	6	7	8	9
10	11	12	13	14	15	16
17	18	19	20	21	22	23
24	25	26	27	28	29	30

NOVEMBER						
S	M	T	W	T	F	S
			1	2	3	4
5	6	7	8	9	10	11
12	13	14	15	16	17	18
19	20	21	22	23	24	25
26	27	28	29	30		

Halloween is the Eve of All Saints' Day.

All Saints' day is the day people go to cemeteries to put flowers on graves. They do this to show they remember their loved ones who have died.

All Saints' Day was at one time called All Hallow's Day.

We got the word *Halloween* from the words of All Hallow's Day.

Hallow is an old English word that means saint, to respect, or something holy about God or Heaven.

A long, long time ago, people believed the dead came out of their graves on the Eve of All Hallow's Day and walked around on the earth.

The colors of Halloween are black and orange.

Halloween celebrations are at night in the fall of the year. The black color of Halloween reminds us of the dark night.

The orange color of Halloween reminds us of the orange fall crop colors, such as pumpkins and persimmons. The orange color reminds us of the big harvest moon that shines in October.

A MEDIEVAL TIMELINE

Each line represents one hundred years A.D.
A.D. ("in the year of the Lord") means after the time of Christ.

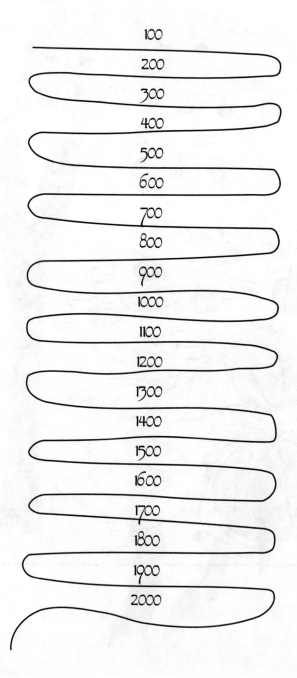

100
200
300
400
500
600
700
800
900
1000
1100
1200
1300
1400
1500
1600
1700
1800
1900
2000

The Celts lived in the British Isles.

The British Isles are the countries of England, Scotland, Wales, and Ireland

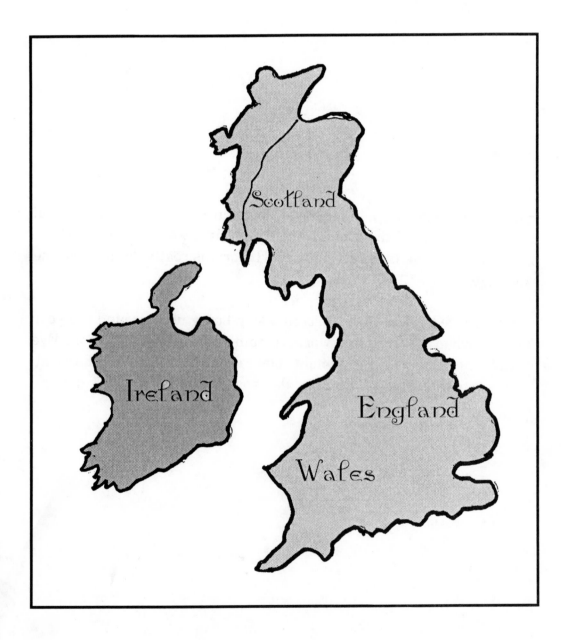

Halloween began back in medieval times with the Celts. The medieval time was also called the Middle Ages. This time was from about the fifth century to the fifteenth century. Historians really do not give the exact dates.

It is believed the word *Halloween* began being used around the year 700 A.D. when the Christian world combined the celebration of the Eve of All Saints' Day with the ancient celebration of the Samhain Festival. At this time in history All Saints' day was called All Hallow's day.

The Celts believed their gods became angry with them at this time of year, because the plants died and it stayed dark for a longer time during the day. They believed the sun god was angry with them because the weather began to turn cold. People at this time in history did not know anything about science. They did not know about the rotation of the earth or how the seasons changed.

The Celts in ancient times, long before the word Halloween was created, had a fall festival called Samhain (SAH-win).

Samhain was the name they gave to their God of darkness and death. Samhain means the summer's end. At their festival they had a big feast. At their feast they ate all of the kinds of foods that were raised during the summer.

The people wanted to do something to make their gods happy. They wanted to give them gifts. They would give sacrifices of food as gifts to their gods. They would do this by building large fires called Samhain fires.

They would throw meat, fruit, and vegetables into the fire from their fall harvest. They believed that as these things burned the rising smoke would deliver their gifts to their gods. This is called pagan worship. A long time ago people did not have churches as we have today, so they worshipped the sun, moon, stars, and sea.

The Irish people called their priests Druids.

The Celtic boys would go from house to house asking for firewood to take to the priests so they could build their Samhain fall festival fires. The firelight was to bring in good spirits and to drive the bad spirits away. The priests would offer the spirits good things to eat. The Druids would dress in costumes so the spirits would not recognize them. This helped develop the custom of "Trick or Treating" and dressing up for Halloween.

The people from Ireland came from the Celts.

The Irish people brought to America their Halloween customs.

They came to America on ships.

Each ship had the flag of Ireland flying high above its mast. The Irish flag colors are green, white, and orange.

17

The story of the Jack-O-Lantern is an Irish Tale.

Once upon a time there was a man named Jack who lived in Ireland. He would not share anything. He was so very stingy. He was so stingy that no one wanted him around. He had tricked the devil many times. When he died, he could not go to heaven or hell. God did not want him. The devil did not want him. The devil told Jack he would have to take a lantern and roam around the earth forever with no special place to live. The devil tossed him a coal of fire. Jack hollowed out a turnip and put the coal of fire in it to use as a lantern to light his way as he walked about the earth.

He was given the name of Jack-O-Lantern.

The Irish people carved faces on turnips to frighten Jack away from their homes. They used turnips because pumpkins did not grow in Ireland.

When they came to America, they used the nice, big, round orange pumpkins and called them Jack-O-Lanterns.

In Ireland the people went "a-souling" on All Hallow's Eve.

They would go from house to house asking for soul cakes. When they ate the soul cakes, it was believed the dead would not suffer and this would help get them to heaven. This was another custom the Irish people brought to America that helped develop the idea of going Trick-or-Treating on Halloween.

The Irish people believed in witches. Witch is an old English word for wise woman. Witches were at one time well-loved people. They knew of ways to heal the sick.

Witches knew which plants made good medicine. They knew how to make medicines.

Witches knew the secrets of nature. They knew magic.

They knew about the signs of the sun, moon, and stars. This is called astrology.

29

Witches would have secret meetings in the woods. They would meet in the woods because some people did not like their witchcraft practices. They dressed in black clothes so they could not be seen. Witches wore the tall hats because that was the style of hat all women wore during medieval time. They would do a broomstick dance by leaping over fires on a broom. They thought they were flying.

Witches love cats. They always have a pet cat. It was believed a witch could change herself into a cat whenever she wanted to.

The black cat became known as a Halloween animal because the witches would bring their black cats to their meetings in the woods, the black bats would fly around, and the owls would screech and hoot. Black cats, bats, and owls became known as Halloween animals because they came out at night to the witches' meetings.

Halloween is a fun time to dress up. We can be anything we want to be on Halloween Night. We can dress up like anyone we want to. A long time ago in medieval times, the people dressed in costumes to drive the evil spirits away.

The autumn leaves, cornstalks, apples, and nuts are part of the Halloween season, reminding us of the Irish Autumn Festival.

So, this is why we have Halloween, because a long, long, time ago the Bible had not been printed so everyone could have a copy. The printing press had not been invented and everything had to be written by hand. People did not have copies of the Bible in their homes as we do today. They did not know about the real God that created the world and universe. They made up stories—called superstitions—about the weather changes. We know their stories were just make-believe and not any of these old myths are true.

Witches, ghosts, and goblins are like elves and fairies; they live only in our imagination.

HALLOWEEN VOCABULARY

Halloween
October
thirty-first
eve
All Saints' Day
cemetery
graves
flowers
English
God
Heaven
died
roamed
around
earth
black
orange
celebrations
night
Autumn
Fall

crops
pumpkins
persimmons
shines
moon
medieval
Celts
century
flying
fifteenth
British Isles
Scotland
Wales
Ireland
Irish
festival
Samhain
darkness
sacrifices
priests
Druids

fires
costumes
custom
jack-o-lantern
share
stingy
devil
witch
Hell
soul
secrets
magic
moon
sun
stars
astrology
witchcraft
broom
broomstick

A HALLOWEEN CHANT

Old Mrs. Witch, Old Mrs. Witch,
Tell me what you see,
Tell me what you see.

I see a little Jack-O-Lantern,
Looking at me.

Old Mrs. Witch, Old Mrs. Witch,
Tell me what you do,
Tell me what you do.

I fly on a broom stick,
And I scare you! BOO!

WITCHES' BREW

1 package orange Kool-Aid
1 cup sugar or sweeten to taste
2 quarts water
1 tall can pineapple juice
1 large can crushed pineapple
1 gallon bag of ice
1 package gummy worms

Add: 1 large bottle of ginger ale just before serving to make fizz.
This may also be served as a hot drink, but leave out the gummy worms
and the ginger ale.

Halloween Art Activities

Make a Jack-O-Lantern out of a paper bag. Stuff the bag with newspaper. Tie bag at top with string or yarn. Twist the top before you tie it. Each student is to be creative, as they are to cut out eyes, nose, and mouth of their own design using orange or black construction paper to paste on their Jack-O-Lantern. Glue really works the best.

The size bag you use depends on how large you want to make the Jack-O-Lanterns.

Make a Pine Cone Owl. Stuff pine cones with cotton balls. Pull cotton balls over pine cone to make a thin layer of cotton to look like down. Students are to be creative by designing their own eyes, beak, and feet out of construction paper. The construction paper will glue to the cotton.

Make Halloween Lanterns out of orange or black construction paper. Fold paper in half. Hold it up like a taco shell and cut, beginning where the fold is. Cut small strips across the paper, leaving about an inch at the top to keep lantern from falling apart. Open the cut work and now make a cylinder shape of it to form the lantern. Glue on matching handle made from construction paper. The handle should be about one-half inch wide, or you can use yarn to make the handle.

Make a Haunted House. Cut house out of black construction paper. Paste onto large sheet of dark blue construction paper. Draw scene around house. Paste white ghosts in windows of house and all around the picture.

Make a Pumpkin Man out of a paper plate. Cut arms and legs out of construction paper. Fold in accordian fashion. Paste hands, feet, and face onto man. Use on orange plate and green construction paper for the arms and legs.